YOUR KNOWLEDGE HAS VALUE

- We will publish your bachelor's and master's thesis, essays and papers

- Your own eBook and book - sold worldwide in all relevant shops

- Earn money with each sale

Upload your text at www.GRIN.com
and publish for free

Bibliographic information published by the German National Library:

The German National Library lists this publication in the National Bibliography; detailed bibliographic data are available on the Internet at http://dnb.dnb.de .

This book is copyright material and must not be copied, reproduced, transferred, distributed, leased, licensed or publicly performed or used in any way except as specifically permitted in writing by the publishers, as allowed under the terms and conditions under which it was purchased or as strictly permitted by applicable copyright law. Any unauthorized distribution or use of this text may be a direct infringement of the author s and publisher s rights and those responsible may be liable in law accordingly.

Imprint:

Copyright © 2017 GRIN Verlag, Open Publishing GmbH
Print and binding: Books on Demand GmbH, Norderstedt Germany
ISBN: 9783668513198

This book at GRIN:

http://www.grin.com/en/e-book/373555/a-generator-for-volatile-demand-profiles-a-brief-description-of-a-tool

Maik Günther

A Generator for Volatile Demand Profiles. A Brief Description of a Tool

GRIN Publishing

GRIN - Your knowledge has value

Since its foundation in 1998, GRIN has specialized in publishing academic texts by students, college teachers and other academics as e-book and printed book. The website www.grin.com is an ideal platform for presenting term papers, final papers, scientific essays, dissertations and specialist books.

Visit us on the internet:

http://www.grin.com/

http://www.facebook.com/grincom

http://www.twitter.com/grin_com

A Generator for Volatile Demand Profiles

Dr. Maik Günther

Working Paper 07/17
July 2017, Munich (Germany)

1 Introduction

To test, compare and improve algorithms and new approaches for staff scheduling, planning problems are needed. Such problems are often not available in literature. Therefore, the Demand Generator was developed to create own problems for staff scheduling. The actual parameters of this tool are based on real data of a call center, which were only slightly modified for the purpose of data protection of the call center. Nevertheless, the tool can also be used for other industries like retail sector or logistics.

The tool creates for a whole year in hourly resolution values for the staffing demand of a specific workstation or a specific function. Opening hours, holidays, weekdays, min/max staffing levels, stochastic elements, events and weather effects are taken into account by the Demand Generator. Fig. 1 shows an example of the calculated demand for one week.

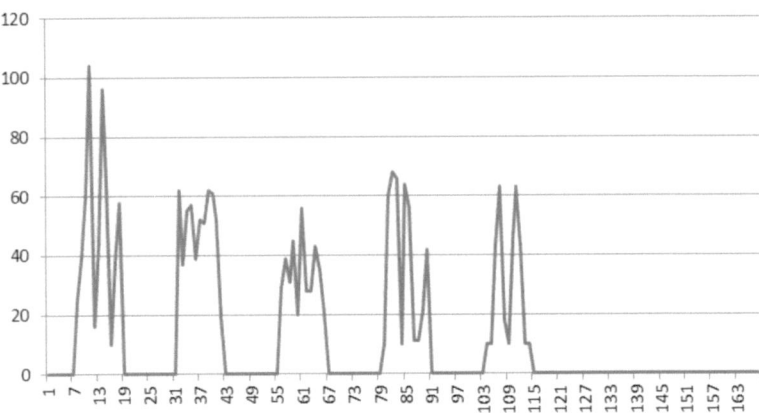

Fig. 1: Final demand of the Demand Generator for a week in hourly resolution.

The Demand Generator is public available and it is allowed to modify it. If the tool or a modified version of the tool is used for a publication, reference should be made to this working paper:

Günther, M.: A Generator for Volatile Demand Profiles, Working Paper 07/17, Munich: GRIN, 2017.

The Demand Generator was developed with MS EXCEL™ and Visual Basic. It can be downloaded at:

http://www.maik-günther.de/DemandGenerator.xlsm

If there are any problems with the 'ü' in the URL, please use the following link:

http://www.xn--maik-gnther-yhb.de/DemandGenerator.xlsm

1 Function of the Demand Generator

The Demand Generator was developed in MS EXCEL and Visual Basic and works in the following way:

1. A deterministic core of the hourly demand is given. These values can be modified by the user of the tool. Without any other modifications this demand is used for each day of the year. Opening hours are taken into account if a 0 is used for the demand. Fig. 2 shows an example for the deterministic core with opening hours from 8 AM till 6 PM.

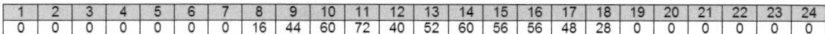

1	2	3	4	5	6	7	8	9	10	11	12	13	14	15	16	17	18	19	20	21	22	23	24
0	0	0	0	0	0	0	16	44	60	72	40	52	60	56	56	48	28	0	0	0	0	0	0

Fig. 2: Deterministic core for 24 hours of each day.

2. There are often differences between the overall demand of weekdays. If a shop or a call center is closed on Sunday weekday factors can be used to set all demand values to 0 at each Saturday of the year (here a weekday factor of -100). Other effects like an increased number of calls on Mondays in comparison to Fridays can also be modeled with weekday factors. Based on the weekday factors the deterministic core will be changed for all days of the year. Fig. 3 shows an example of weekday factors. These values can be modified by the user.

weekday	change in %
Monday	20,00
Tuesday	10,00
Wednesday	0,00
Thursday	-10,00
Friday	-20,00
Saturday	-100,00
Sunday	-100,00

Fig. 3: Weekday factors.

3. The Demand Generator can also use events which influence the demand of specific days. Such events are often planned by the marketing departments. Other types of events are for example holidays, weather effects, important football games, etc. The user is free to create own events with own specific effects. Examples are given in Fig. 4.

name of the event	change in %	abbr.
holiday	-20	F
bridging day	5	B
event (price adjustment) day 1	5	P1
event (price adjustment) day 2	10	P2
event (price adjustment) day 3	30	P3
event (price adjustment) day 4	30	P4
event (price adjustment) day 5	20	P5
Event20	20	E20
Event30	30	E30
Event50	50	E50

Fig. 4: Definition of events.

After events are defined, they can be assigned to the days of the year. It is possible to assign more than one event to a day. Fig. 5 shows an example. Here the event P1 (the first day of a price adjustment) is assigned to the day with the number 337. As a result the demand from step 2 will be modified according the assigned events.

A Generator for Volatile Demand Profiles

number of the day	event
337	P1
338	P2
339	P3
340	P4
341	P5
64	E20
65	E30
66	E20
169	E20
170	E20

Fig. 5: Assignment of events to days.

4. To take stochastic effects into account an Ornstein-Uhlenbeck process can be added to the result of the previous step. The user can choose own parameters for the Ornstein-Uhlenbeck process. The preselected parameters are presented in Fig. 6.

parameters for the Ornstein-Uhlenbeck process		
	δ	41,30
	λ	1,87
	μ	0,00

Fig. 6: Parameters of the Ornstein-Uhlenbeck process.

5. If the hourly values of the demand should be limited, an upper and lower bound can be given (see Fig. 7 for an example).

min number in final demand	10
max number in final demand	1000

Fig. 7: Min/max levels of the final demand.

Checkboxes are available to activate or deactivate the steps 2-5 (see Fig. 8). It is possible to deactivate all checkboxes and to run the model. The result will be the deterministic core at all days of the year without any modifications.

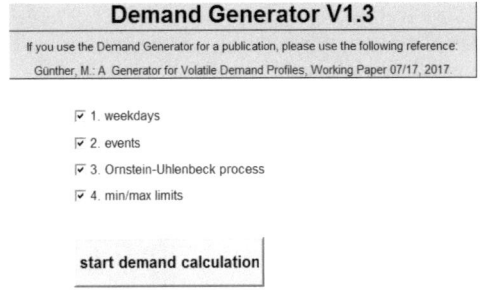

Fig. 8: Check boxes and the start button of the demand generator.

The output of the calculation is given in two ways.

- One table with 168 columns (hours from Monday till Sunday) and 52 rows (weeks of a year).

A Generator for Volatile Demand Profiles

- A second table below the first table with 24 columns (hours of a day) and 260 rows (days of a year without Saturday and Sunday).

Fig. 9 shows an example of the first table. Due to the limited space, only results of each Monday of weeks 1-44 are shown in Fig. 9. If a different format for the output is needed the Visual Basic source code has to be changed by the user (the source code is presented in the appendix of this paper).

week	\multicolumn{24}{c	}{Monday}
	1	2	3	4	5	6	7	8	9	10	11	12	13	14	15	16	17	18	19	20	21	22	23	24
1	0	0	0	0	0	0	0	23	47	52	41	42	53	56	71	82	51	10	0	0	0	0	0	0
2	0	0	0	0	0	0	0	10	64	55	41	49	108	57	50	40	73	10	0	0	0	0	0	0
3	0	0	0	0	0	0	0	10	64	88	113	19	36	103	74	53	61	47	0	0	0	0	0	0
4	0	0	0	0	0	0	0	16	24	50	94	43	34	80	97	62	44	11	0	0	0	0	0	0
5	0	0	0	0	0	0	0	34	75	56	85	52	84	55	48	86	83	28	0	0	0	0	0	0
6	0	0	0	0	0	0	0	16	67	68	73	40	100	68	52	64	73	22	0	0	0	0	0	0
7	0	0	0	0	0	0	0	10	61	74	83	33	45	89	74	51	74	40	0	0	0	0	0	0
8	0	0	0	0	0	0	0	23	47	44	90	51	60	89	95	72	23	25	0	0	0	0	0	0
9	0	0	0	0	0	0	0	34	36	28	87	94	47	55	40	82	34	10	0	0	0	0	0	0
10	0	0	0	0	0	0	0	41	81	113	74	32	105	93	66	83	83	47	0	0	0	0	0	0
11	0	0	0	0	0	0	0	10	31	80	81	20	70	102	62	53	35	99	0	0	0	0	0	0
12	0	0	0	0	0	0	0	39	36	71	90	70	45	53	86	92	52	41	0	0	0	0	0	0
13	0	0	0	0	0	0	0	30	38	45	61	76	46	43	51	69	34	10	0	0	0	0	0	0
14	0	0	0	0	0	0	0	36	58	72	64	33	81	78	51	82	59	46	0	0	0	0	0	0
15	0	0	0	0	0	0	0	12	25	76	89	46	79	100	72	32	49	72	0	0	0	0	0	0
16	0	0	0	0	0	0	0	10	10	73	132	33	45	45	82	43	30	43	0	0	0	0	0	0
17	0	0	0	0	0	0	0	33	80	43	60	79	69	58	70	80	64	19	0	0	0	0	0	0
18	0	0	0	0	0	0	0	10	61	67	58	56	92	67	53	44	123	32	0	0	0	0	0	0
19	0	0	0	0	0	0	0	10	52	76	108	31	43	91	92	61	65	67	0	0	0	0	0	0
20	0	0	0	0	0	0	0	13	39	64	124	44	47	69	82	55	10	12	0	0	0	0	0	0
21	0	0	0	0	0	0	0	28	56	53	64	49	70	55	82	67	65	10	0	0	0	0	0	0
22	0	0	0	0	0	0	0	10	46	61	67	55	78	63	19	45	84	32	0	0	0	0	0	0
23	0	0	0	0	0	0	0	10	54	118	71	31	35	87	43	39	67	62	0	0	0	0	0	0
24	0	0	0	0	0	0	0	44	24	46	117	55	48	75	80	73	43	10	0	0	0	0	0	0
25	0	0	0	0	0	0	0	34	60	59	111	88	69	72	57	145	68	31	0	0	0	0	0	0
26	0	0	0	0	0	0	0	21	57	94	69	29	81	97	61	74	91	62	0	0	0	0	0	0
27	0	0	0	0	0	0	0	10	45	110	82	33	59	87	55	11	36	52	0	0	0	0	0	0
28	0	0	0	0	0	0	0	31	48	67	117	68	59	100	80	86	24	27	0	0	0	0	0	0
29	0	0	0	0	0	0	0	28	57	70	103	76	67	37	58	105	63	10	0	0	0	0	0	0
30	0	0	0	0	0	0	0	27	100	57	69	21	77	48	39	76	86	106	0	0	0	0	0	0
31	0	0	0	0	0	0	0	10	15	89	76	24	53	71	60	39	21	41	0	0	0	0	0	0
32	0	0	0	0	0	0	0	10	14	66	99	33	36	35	119	52	36	26	0	0	0	0	0	0
33	0	0	0	0	0	0	0	19	64	41	50	57	75	52	61	87	74	27	0	0	0	0	0	0
34	0	0	0	0	0	0	0	10	80	54	54	35	65	46	10	32	64	10	0	0	0	0	0	0
35	0	0	0	0	0	0	0	10	37	89	88	35	78	71	73	20	39	40	0	0	0	0	0	0
36	0	0	0	0	0	0	0	18	40	75	97	43	15	49	92	59	17	47	0	0	0	0	0	0
37	0	0	0	0	0	0	0	61	27	41	42	53	26	30	63	82	118	14	0	0	0	0	0	0
38	0	0	0	0	0	0	0	10	85	79	72	51	75	78	52	42	72	40	0	0	0	0	0	0
39	0	0	0	0	0	0	0	10	61	102	81	34	39	137	65	57	57	45	0	0	0	0	0	0
40	0	0	0	0	0	0	0	40	36	53	105	73	56	79	100	95	58	15	0	0	0	0	0	0
41	0	0	0	0	0	0	0	62	60	71	100	73	62	30	58	98	51	37	0	0	0	0	0	0
42	0	0	0	0	0	0	0	15	84	92	83	76	75	91	33	60	71	55	0	0	0	0	0	0
43	0	0	0	0	0	0	0	16	70	100	91	13	53	110	72	38	78	45	0	0	0	0	0	0
44	0	0	0	0	0	0	0	10	24	31	84	14	22	67	82	126	33	22	0	0	0	0	0	0
45	0	0	0	0	0	0	0	54	60	58	89	61	68	57	42	81	64	18	0	0	0	0	0	0
46	0	0	0	0	0	0	0	31	83	68	72	25	127	70	57	66	69	20	0	0	0	0	0	0
47	0	0	0	0	0	0	0	10	34	91	111	42	69	105	95	67	39	37	0	0	0	0	0	0
48	0	0	0	0	0	0	0	10	37	69	101	36	10	50	85	48	54	38	0	0	0	0	0	0
49	0	0	0	0	0	0	0	51	76	73	118	63	84	42	63	83	82	24	0	0	0	0	0	0
50	0	0	0	0	0	0	0	36	81	77	51	39	100	77	38	87	69	33	0	0	0	0	0	0
51	0	0	0	0	0	0	0	10	27	87	62	20	71	100	139	54	53	37	0	0	0	0	0	0
52	0	0	0	0	0	0	0	17	27	60	82	44	35	33	68	90	35	35	0	0	0	0	0	0

Fig. 9: Results of the Demand Generator.

The user can also use the results of the Demand Generator to derive own demand data, if the results are only interpreted as demand drivers. Such demand drivers can be incoming calls, customers, packages, tasks, etc. Based on these demand drivers the demand for personnel scheduling in hourly resolution can be derived in a separate step (not part of the Demand Generator). An example should illustrate this: Let's assume that the Demand Generator calculates 70 inbound calls in hour 8 of a specific day. If a call center agent can handle on average 7 inbound calls per hour, 10 agents are needed in hour 8 to cover the demand. If a call center has only 9 workplaces, the number of needed agent in hour 8 is limited to 9.

5

A Generator for Volatile Demand Profiles

Appendix – Visual Basic source code

```
Option Explicit

Public t, y, s, z As Integer          'counter for loops
Public MinNumber As Integer
Public MaxNumber As Integer
Public Vola As Single                 'volatility
Public Lambda As Single               'lambda
Public My As Single                   'mean value

Private DEMANDresult(1 To 8760) As Integer          'array for final demand
Private DEMANDdeterministic(1 To 8760) As Integer   'array for deterministic core
Private DEMANDstochastic(1 To 8760) As Single       'array for stochastic demand

Private Sub CommandButton1_Click()
    Application.ScreenUpdating = False

    PrepareArrays
    ReadData
    CreateDemand
    Output

    Application.ScreenUpdating = True
End Sub

Function PrepareArrays()
    Erase DEMANDresult
    Erase DEMANDdeterministic
    Erase DEMANDstochastic
End Function

Function ReadData()
    MinNumber = Cells(41, 2).value
    MaxNumber = Cells(42, 2).value
    Vola = Cells(36, 2).value
    Lambda = Cells(37, 2).value
    My = Cells(38, 2).value

    'read deterministic core
    y = 0
    For t = 1 To (24 * 364)
        DEMANDdeterministic(t) = Cells(32, 6 + y).value
        y = y + 1
        If y = 24 Then y = 0
    Next t
End Function

Function CreateDemand()
    'weekdays
    If CBool(CheckBox1.value) Then
```

A Generator for Volatile Demand Profiles

```
    z = 1
    y = 1
    For t = 1 To (24 * 364)
        '1st day is a Monday in 2018
        DEMANDdeterministic(t) = DEMANDdeterministic(t) * (1 + (Cells(58 + z, 2).value) / 100)
        y = y + 1
        If y = 25 Then
            z = z + 1
            y = 1
        End If
        If z = 8 Then z = 1
    Next t
End If

'events
If CBool(CheckBox2.value) Then
    For t = 1 To 500
        If Cells(68 + t, 2).value = "F" Then
            For z = 1 To 24
                DEMANDdeterministic((Cells(68 + t, 1).value - 1) * 24 + z) =
                    DEMANDdeterministic((Cells(68 + t, 1).value - 1) * 24 + z) * (1 + Cells(46, 2).value / 100)
            Next z
        End If
        If Cells(68 + t, 2).value = "B" Then
            For z = 1 To 24
                DEMANDdeterministic((Cells(68 + t, 1).value - 1) * 24 + z) =
                    DEMANDdeterministic((Cells(68 + t, 1).value - 1) * 24 + z) * (1 + Cells(47, 2).value / 100)
            Next z
        End If
        If Cells(68 + t, 2).value = "P1" Then
            For z = 1 To 24
                DEMANDdeterministic((Cells(68 + t, 1).value - 1) * 24 + z) =
                    DEMANDdeterministic((Cells(68 + t, 1).value - 1) * 24 + z) * (1 + Cells(48, 2).value / 100)
            Next z
        End If
        If Cells(68 + t, 2).value = "P2" Then
            For z = 1 To 24
                DEMANDdeterministic((Cells(68 + t, 1).value - 1) * 24 + z) =
                    DEMANDdeterministic((Cells(68 + t, 1).value - 1) * 24 + z) * (1 + Cells(49, 2).value / 100)
            Next z
        End If
        If Cells(68 + t, 2).value = "P3" Then
            For z = 1 To 24
                DEMANDdeterministic((Cells(68 + t, 1).value - 1) * 24 + z) =
                    DEMANDdeterministic((Cells(68 + t, 1).value - 1) * 24 + z) * (1 + Cells(50, 2).value / 100)
            Next z
        End If
        If Cells(68 + t, 2).value = "P4" Then
            For z = 1 To 24
                DEMANDdeterministic((Cells(68 + t, 1).value - 1) * 24 + z) =
                    DEMANDdeterministic((Cells(68 + t, 1).value - 1) * 24 + z) * (1 + Cells(51, 2).value / 100)
            Next z
```

```
            End If
            If Cells(68 + t, 2).value = "P5" Then
                For z = 1 To 24
                    DEMANDdeterministic((Cells(68 + t, 1).value - 1) * 24 + z) =
                        DEMANDdeterministic((Cells(68 + t, 1).value - 1) * 24 + z) * (1 + Cells(52, 2).value / 100)
                Next z
            End If
            If Cells(68 + t, 2).value = "E20" Then
                For z = 1 To 24
                    DEMANDdeterministic((Cells(68 + t, 1).value - 1) * 24 + z) =
                        DEMANDdeterministic((Cells(68 + t, 1).value - 1) * 24 + z) * (1 + Cells(53, 2).value / 100)
                Next z
            End If
            If Cells(68 + t, 2).value = "E30" Then
                For z = 1 To 24
                    DEMANDdeterministic((Cells(68 + t, 1).value - 1) * 24 + z) =
                        DEMANDdeterministic((Cells(68 + t, 1).value - 1) * 24 + z) * (1 + Cells(54, 2).value / 100)
                Next z
            End If
            If Cells(68 + t, 2).value = "E50" Then
                For z = 1 To 24
                    DEMANDdeterministic((Cells(68 + t, 1).value - 1) * 24 + z) =
                        DEMANDdeterministic((Cells(68 + t, 1).value - 1) * 24 + z) * (1 + Cells(55, 2).value / 100)
                Next z
            End If
        Next t
    End If

    'Ornstein-Uhlenbeck process
    If CBool(CheckBox3.value) Then
        DEMANDstochastic(1) = 0
        Dim Zufallszahl1 As Double
        Dim Zufallszahl2 As Double

        For t = 2 To (24 * 364)
            If DEMANDdeterministic(t) > 0 Then 'only if demand at the deterministic core > 0
                Randomize Timer
                Zufallszahl1 = Rnd() 'random number
                Zufallszahl2 = Rnd() 'random number
                Zufallszahl1 = (-2 * Log(Zufallszahl1)) ^ 0.5 * Cos(2 * 3.14159265358979 * Zufallszahl2)

                DEMANDstochastic(t) = DEMANDstochastic(t - 1) * Exp(1) ^ (-Lambda) + My * (1 - Exp(1) ^
                    (-Lambda)) + Zufallszahl1 * Vola * ((1 - Exp(1) ^ (-2 * Lambda)) / (2 * Lambda)) ^ 0.5
            End If
        Next t
    End If

    'add stochastic part to the deterministic part
    For t = 1 To (24 * 364)
        DEMANDresult(t) = DEMANDstochastic(t) + DEMANDdeterministic(t)
    Next t
```

A Generator for Volatile Demand Profiles

```
'min/max limits
If CBool(CheckBox4.value) Then
   For t = 1 To (24 * 364)
      If DEMANDdeterministic(t) > 0 Then
         If DEMANDresult(t) < MinNumber Then DEMANDresult(t) = MinNumber
         If DEMANDresult(t) > MaxNumber Then DEMANDresult(t) = MaxNumber
      End If
   Next t
End If

'rounding to integer values
For t = 1 To (24 * 364)
   DEMANDresult(t) = Math.Round(DEMANDresult(t), 0)
Next t
End Function

Function Output()
'output with 7 days per week; each week a separate line
s = 0
z = 0
For t = 1 To (24 * 364)
   Cells(40 + z, 6 + s) = DEMANDresult(t)
   s = s + 1
   If s = (7 * 24) Then
      s = 0
      z = z + 1
   End If
Next t

'output with 5 days per week; each day a separate line
s = 0
z = 0
y = 0
For t = 1 To (24 * 364)
   Cells(98 + z, 6 + s) = DEMANDresult(t)
   s = s + 1
   If s = (1 * 24) Then
      y = y + 1
      s = 0
      z = z + 1
   End If
   If y = 5 Then 'only 5 days
      y = 0
      t = t + (2 * 24) 'ignore 2 days (Saturday and Sunday)
   End If
Next t
End Function
```

YOUR KNOWLEDGE HAS VALUE

- We will publish your bachelor's and master's thesis, essays and papers

- Your own eBook and book - sold worldwide in all relevant shops

- Earn money with each sale

Upload your text at www.GRIN.com and publish for free